From Caves to Castles

Pamela Graham

1998 Barrie Publishing Pty Limited
From Caves to Castles
Text copyright © Pamela Graham
Illustrations copyright © Ian Forss

Momentum program © Barrie Publishing Pty Limited

All rights reserved.
No part of this book may be reproduced, stored in a retrieval system, or transmitted in any form or by any means, electronic, mechanical, photocopying, recording or otherwise, without prior permission of the copyright owner.

Published by Troll Communications L.L.C.
Reprinted by arrangement with Barrie Publishing Pty Limited, Suite 513, 89 High Street, Kew, Australia, 3101

ISBN 0 8167 4993 0

Printed in Singapore by PH Productions Pte Ltd
10 9 8 7 6 5 4 3 2 1

Every effort has been made to contact the owners of the photographs in this book. Where this has not been possible, we invite the owners of the copyright to notify the publishers.

ANT Photo Library/J.Burt p. 7; ANT Photo Library/Peter McDonald pp. 11, 19; ANT Photo Library/N.H.P.A. p. 5; ANT Photo Library/ J. O'Neil p. 6; ANT Photo Library/Otto Rogge p. 18; ANT Photo Library/Silvestris cover, pp. 1, 20, 22; ANT Photo Library/ R. Thwaites p. 17; Horizon Photo Library pp. 12-13; International Photographic Library p. 15; Northside Photographics pp. 14 (insert), 21; Northside Photographics/Brian Carroll p. 14; Phil Norton/Painet Stock p. 10; Bill Thomas p. 4; Marilyn Wynn/Painet Stock p. 16.

Contents

The First Shelters 4

Homes from Bits and Pieces 7

Portable Houses 10

Disposable Houses 14

Dwellings to Stay 17

Glossary 23

Index 24

The First Shelters

Caves were most likely the first shelters prehistoric people used. Caves gave protection from the wind and rain. They were cool in summer. In winter, fires kept them warm. Fires at the entrance also kept out most wild animals.

Some people settled in caves or under rock overhangs. They could live in a cave all year round if there was plenty of food and fresh water nearby. They moved away only when weather conditions or lack of food forced them to.

African tribesmen making string outside their hut.

Many early humans did not settle in one place. They moved around, gathering seasonal food. Sometimes, they followed migrating animals. These people tended to make temporary shelters, because they were often on the move.

The women in the African tribes of the San, for instance, gathered branches and grass to make temporary huts. They built the huts, too. These huts gave shelter from the sun and the wind. They kept rain out and provided a place to keep belongings. They were not very high, and the people could not stand upright inside. They were not sleeping places unless the weather was bad. The San preferred to sleep outdoors.

The Australian Aboriginal people also made temporary shelters. Their *gunyahs* were made of boughs and bark. Sometimes, a tree was used as a support for the other material. In different parts of Australia, a shelter was also called a *mia-mia* or *wurley*. In tropical areas where rainfall was heavy, some people built grass-covered homes, something like an igloo. The rain ran off the thick layers of grass. The inside stayed dry. People couldn't stand up in these shelters, either.

Homes from Bits and Pieces

As people moved to new areas, they built their homes from any materials that were available. Bamboo, leaves, grass, wool, animal skins and bones, moss, reeds, snow and ice, and even cow dung, have all been used as building materials.

The people living across northern Asia at the end of the Ice Age used animal bones as the frames for their homes. They couldn't use branches or bark, because there were no trees. The rib bones of the huge mammoth were used as posts. They were pushed into the ground in a circle. They were then covered by the dried skin of the mammoth. To kill animals such as the mammoth, the people dug big pit-traps. When an animal fell into the pit, it landed on sharpened stakes. People also made use of animals that had died of natural causes.

The mammoth provided most of the people's needs. Besides the rib bones and skin used for shelters, the meat was used for food, the skin was used for clothes, and some bones for tools. Awls and needles, cutting tools and scrapers were made from the bones. Fat from the animal was boiled down and used as a fuel to light lamps.

Portable Houses

In some parts of the world, people took their homes with them instead of building new shelters each time they moved.

Some of the Native Americans followed the migrating bison, or American buffalo. These animals provided food as well as material for housing. Hides were sewn together as a covering for a tepee.

The tepee was a cone-shaped tent that stood tall. As it was wide at the base, it was quite roomy. Long poles made the framework. These poles were covered with buffalo hides that were held down with pegs. A hole at the top, where the poles crossed, let out hot air and smoke from the inside fires. The entrance was an opening flap.

   As many as 20 hides might be needed for one tepee. These were often decorated with special designs. Hides were also used as flooring. When the herds of buffalo moved, the people could collapse their tepees. They would use large dogs, then horses, to drag the tepees to the next place where they set up camp.

Some people in the present day still use portable housing. The Tuareg people roam over the vast Sahara Desert in North Africa. Their homes are long tents. To set up the tents, ropes are lashed to supporting poles. The ropes are then pinned to the ground by pegs. More poles and ropes are added to make the tents larger. Coverings thrown over the frames are made from goatskins or sometimes camel skins.

The coverings are thick enough to protect against the hot sun. The sides can be rolled up from the ground to let the breeze in. They can be lowered to keep out wind and sand.

Although the desert is hot in the daytime, it can be very cold at night. The people sit around small fires to cook their food and to keep warm.

These homes are easily taken down and rolled up. They are loaded onto camels for the move to the next site.

Disposable Houses

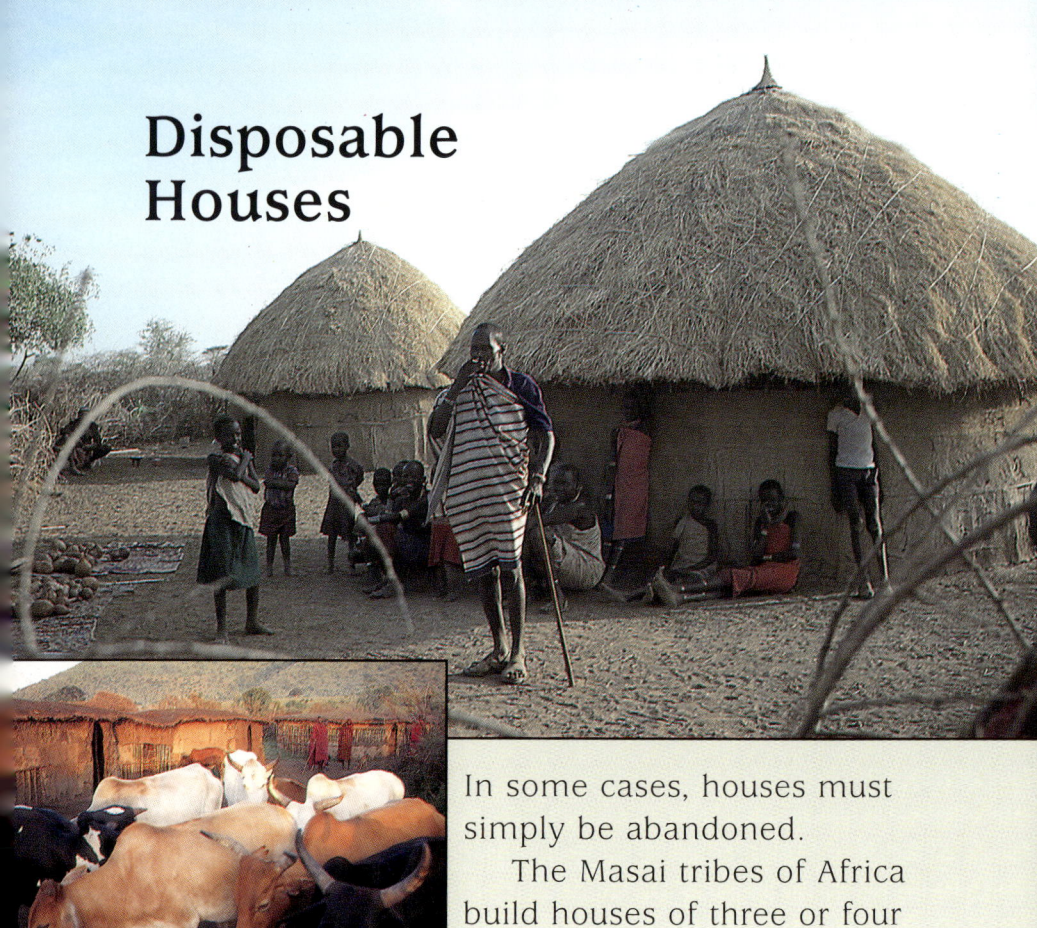

In some cases, houses must simply be abandoned.

The Masai tribes of Africa build houses of three or four rooms. The walls are made of cow dung mixed with mud. When this dries, it is rock hard. The houses have a dome-shaped thatched roof. A hole in the top lets out smoke from the inside fire. A curved entrance keeps out wind and rain. It also keeps out animals.

Although these houses are permanent, the people often move. The Masai's wealth is in their herds of cattle. If pastures are better in another area, the people move and build new houses.

In the Arctic, some Inuit people move with the seasons. They build different types of shelters for winter and summer. In winter, some Inuit people build their homes out of snow. They also build these igloos when they have to travel long distances over snow and ice.

Big blocks are cut from firm snow and placed in a circle. As more blocks are placed on top, they are placed in smaller and smaller circles to form a dome. Some blocks of clear ice are used to let a little light in. A hole at the top lets out smoke from the oil lamps. The entrance is a low tunnel with storage areas.

Another type of winter home is built around a frame of driftwood or whalebone. It is covered by moss and earth to keep out the cold. The entrance is a long, low tunnel. In summer, a tent covered by walrus skin or sealskin is used.

The interior of the summer hut is decorated with rugs and skins.

Dwellings to Stay

As the number of people grew, new ways of providing food were needed. People started to grow crops and keep animals. That meant they could settle in one place. Because they didn't have to travel or search for edible plants, they had more time for building houses. They could make homes that were more permanent.

Among the first permanent building materials were bricks. These bricks were made from mud. When dried in the sun, they lasted a long time. In Africa, mud-brick houses had roofs of thatched grass.

The Pueblo Indians in the southwestern part of the United States built their houses from sun-dried clay bricks called adobe. Sometimes, they used stones cemented together with adobe. Sometimes a house was completely made of the orange-brown clay.

Some early Pueblo Indians built houses against cliffs. These homes were like square boxes. They had few doors and windows. To get inside, a person had to climb a ladder to the roof, then go in by a trapdoor.

Sometimes, other levels were built on top of the first. These were also reached by ladder. Whole communities could be connected this way. In the days when the tribes fought, the ladders were pulled up so the enemy had no way of getting in.

Pueblo towns were not always boxlike in their construction.

The big castles in Europe sometimes held many families. The king gave large areas of land to his lords. In return the lords provided armies to fight for him. Serfs worked the land to provide food. In return for their work and food, the lord gave them protection from enemies by letting them into his castle. These serfs then fought for him and the king.

Some castles were built on a huge mound with steeply sloping sides. Sometimes castles were built on the peak of a ridge. This made it harder for enemies to attack the castles.

The first castles were built of wood and mud. Later, they were built of stone. The main building of the castle was called the keep. Smaller buildings, like the chapel and bakehouse, were grouped together inside the courtyard. A big protective fence or wall was built around the castle. A moat was dug around the outside. A bridge provided access across the moat. The bridge could be drawn up to close the castle.

In times of war, the serfs rushed over the drawbridge into the castle. The drawbridge was then lifted to keep the enemy out.

There were many things people had to think about when building houses. They needed to make houses that suited the conditions in which they lived. They had to use materials that were readily available. The houses they built had to provide protection from the weather and from enemies.

Whether it was a cave or a castle, people lived in the houses that suited them best.

Glossary

awls	pointed tools that are used for making holes in leather
chapel	a private room or building set up especially for prayer or worship
edible	able to be eaten
Ice Age	the most recent period about 2 million to 10,000 years ago, when glaciers spread over large parts of the earth
mammoth	an extinct species related to the modern-day elephant
migrating	going from one area to another
moat	a deep, wide trench that was dug around a castle to stop invaders
permanent	intended to last for a long time
prehistoric	before recorded history
serf	a farm worker who was not allowed to leave the land
temporary	lasting only for a certain period

Index

adobe 18
Africa 14, 17
African tribes 5
animal/animals 5, 8, 9, 10, 14, 17
Arctic 15
Asia 8
Australia 6
Australian Aboriginal people 6
bison 10
bones 7, 8, 9
buffalo 10, 11
castle/castles 20, 21, 22
cave/caves 4, 22
cow dung 7, 14
enemy/enemies 18, 20, 21, 22
entrance 4, 10, 14, 15, 16
Europe 20
fire/fires 4, 10, 13, 14
food 4, 5, 9, 10, 13, 17, 20
frame/frames 8, 12, 16
grass 5, 6, 7, 17
ground 8, 13
gunyahs 6
hole 10, 14, 15
home/homes 6, 7, 8, 10, 12, 13, 15, 16, 17, 18
houses 14, 17, 18, 22
hut/huts 5, 16
ice 7, 15
Ice Age 8
igloo/igloos 6, 15

Inuit 15
mammoth 8, 9
Masai 14
material/materials 6, 7, 10, 17, 22
mia-mia 6
mud 14, 17, 21
Native Americans 10
North Africa 12
poles 10, 12
Pueblo Indians 18
rain 4, 5, 6, 14
roof/roofs 14, 17, 18
Sahara Desert 12
shelter/shelters 4, 5, 6, 9, 10
skin/skins 8, 9, 16
smoke 10, 14, 15
snow 7, 15
stone/stones 18, 21
summer 4, 15, 16
sun 5, 13, 17
tent/tents 10, 12
tepee/tepees 10, 11
Tuareg people 12
tunnel 15, 16
wall/walls 14, 21
weather 4, 22
wind 4, 5, 13, 14
winter 4, 15, 16
wurley 6